unbrained

I0566408

FLOWERSONG
PRESS

by

brenna womer

FLOWERSONG

PRESS

FlowerSong Press
Copyright © 2023 by Brenna Womer
ISBN: 978-1953447-26-5

Published by FlowerSong Press
in the United States of America.
www.flowersongpress.com

Cover Art by Genessis Lopez
Set in Adobe Garamond Pro

NOTICE: SCHOOLS AND BUSINESSES
FlowerSong Press offers copies of this book at quantity
discount with bulk purchase for educational, business, or sales
promotional use. For information, please email the Publisher at
info@flowersongpress.com.

Acknowledgments

Thanks to the editors & staff at the following publications for first putting these pieces into the world:

"cost of living" in *North American Review*
"Sweet Nothings" in *Redivider*
"a room, unfinished" in *Bellingham Review*
"Hunny" in *Pithead Chapel*
"shitty father's day poem" & "al pastor" in *Ligeia Magazine*
"Cat and Mouse" in *Gasher*
"the bath" in *Q/A Poetry*
"paige" in *Pacifica Literary Review*
"Flesh Creep" in *Autofocus*
"Go" in *Sixth Finch*
"piecemeal" in *Juked*
"Rot" in *Oyez Review*
"a liberation" in *Birdcoat Quarterly*
"the weed" in *No Contact*
"I'm here today, and" & "dew claw" in *Gone Lawn*
"It's the end of the world as we know it" in *Cleaver Magazine*
"Distancing" in *Bending Genres*
"when the job you worked your ass off for is given to an older white man with a soul patch, you ask your husband to fuck you with the lights on" in *Free State Review*
"Cape Fair" in *Cimarron Review*
"Unbrained" in *Honey Literary*
"i left your blood on my ankle" in *Yes Poetry*
"Thick Like Me" in *NELLE*

table of contents

In the brain I met someone educated. I spoke to this person who is educated. In the brain I spoke about unbrained things hormones and children nursing and nights without a child in the bed. Sleeping.

—Layli Long Soldier, from "Head Count"

unbrained

cost of living

I came home to a
tax collector; he
wanted to break
my bones, to age me
like a stone, to be
my mother.

I offered him a glass
of milk, and he drank
two; the dog and i
could smell his feet
through his shoes. He
asked for a list:

anything, he said, *that*
might fetch a price, but
you've eaten the last of
your mother's apple pie,
and there's no place, yet,
to sell a memory.

I brought him your
robe, all-gray like fur
and the dog's favorite;
the teaspoon I know

is a teaspoon but doesn't
say so, doesn't have to.

he said, *it's not enough*,
but I told him it has to be.

Sweet Nothings

A sixteen-year-old high school junior goes to Zales in the mall with her boyfriend's mother to pick out the ring she wants him to propose with. Both the girl and the mother know there's only one diamond in the case he can afford—a fourth-carat stone in white gold—so they pretend it's the one the girl wants because, right now, all she wants is a marriage nothing like her parents' and thinks she can have it with him, so she'd say yes to a soda can tab or a Ring Pop or a well-tied loop of string. She'd say yes to nothing. She has her ring finger sized, the mother to report back.

*

A sixteen-year-old high school junior sees her boyfriend's mother's minivan pull into a parking spot in front of her apartment building. His mother lets him out with a bouquet of flowers and a box of ice cream sandwiches in a plastic grocery bag and then leaves. The eighteen-year-old gets down on one knee in the kitchen of the apartment the girl shares with her mother, who listens against the door of her bedroom a few feet away. A decade later, when the girl is a woman, she won't remember what he said in the way of a proposal, just how little they had to say to each other after she said yes, how awkward the silence.

*

A sixteen-year-old high school junior and an eighteen-year-old high school dropout scout a pink B&B in town for their upcoming nuptials. They haven't set a date yet because at least one of them is scared shitless and knows the wedding can never actually happen. At least one of them knows life has to be bigger than this, but is afraid to let go because what if it's not. The sixteen-year-old's mother drove them to the venue, and she peeks around the garden while the couple teeters on the porch swing out front. He's wearing his father's brown-leather flight jacket, and she shoulders an empty purse. The three go inside to ask about availability, and they're handed a brochure by the woman working the front desk, who is polite but understandably dubious. The pamphlet tranquilizes the mother and the couple, and they return to the car through the back garden, where the sixteen-year-old can imagine some version of herself happy.

*

A sixteen-year-old high school junior stands alone in a David's Bridal dressing room, surrounded by cheap, white taffeta. Her mother sits on a stool just outside the door in front of a three-way mirror under fluorescent lights. The sixteen-year-old's hair has been let down from a ponytail, so there's a crease just above her ears, and her makeup is oily and smeared after eight hours of classes. She feels the room is a bit cramped; she feels a bit sick to her stomach; she feels exceptionally alone. She doesn't like any of the dresses the attendant picked out, but really, she doesn't like herself or who she is yet; really, she isn't sure who will ever love her if he stops. And because she can't imagine life too far beyond this moment, she picks a strapless tea-length with horizontal bands that reminds her of the one Julia Roberts wears in *Runaway Bride*, the one she swishes like a bell, and sings, *ding, ding, ding.*

*

A sixteen-year-old high school junior sits cross-legged on the carpet across from her eighteen-year-old fiancé in the basement bedroom of his parents' house. She hands him the chip of a diamond she'd been wearing on her finger for the last three months, the one her science teacher laughed at, saying, "Don't be an idiot," and that her boss said she couldn't wear at work. A decade later she won't remember what she said in the way of a breakup, only that her fear of missing out on more, at some point, started outweighing the security of the moment. He threw the ring across the room but dug it out of a pile of laundry when she left. They'd get back together and break up again, but the ring would remain on his dresser next to a stack of change.

*

A nineteen-year-old college sophomore stands alone in line at UPS, stuffing a never-worn wedding dress into a used cardboard box. She's relieved the dress serves as its own packing material, so she doesn't have to shell out for bubble wrap or Styrofoam peanuts; these days, she has her own rent to pay, and the fifty bucks she got for the dress won't go far, but she's so tired and embarrassed of seeing the reminder of her almost-life in the back corner of her closet that she'd have said yes to thirty, to fifteen; she was so desperate she'd have given it away. She tapes the box shut and writes the address of an eBay buyer on a bright white label.

a room, unfinished

does it end, forgotten darling—
the earth
your rope
what it feels like to know?

everything is a door,
an escape from the light; I
woke up to name the darkness
                    the lavender, parting
                        lakes traced open;
remind my heart of the ground,
that the world turns for the devil just the same.

can we know what is holy,
                 early boy?
                    painter, daydreamer
fire from the womb
     of a child bride,
a mother wed to this earth, to
the dirt, and pronounced
              forever young
by the prince of darkness or
dead leaves

I've lost patience with remembering, and
trust nothing but your open mouth

are we so bitter and blown-out to ask—

                                          is this all there is?

fuck me into silence on the eve

               we lose our shadows,

and light my bones like a candle

so I don't break you in the dark.

are we alone,

       forgotten darling,

              waiting on some blue wound,

looking for the other half of a woman,

sun-hungry   lost   and losing sight?

it's late,

your face is sand,

and we are running out of night.

Hunny

My mother had a parakeet when I was twelve years old, and for a while, she clipped its wings with a pair of kitchen shears. My mother stayed home and, in the early days of Blogger, spent most of her time on the computer with the bird perched atop her head. As she stared at the screen, the bird would lean forward, pressing my mother's bangs flat against her forehead with its feathered chest, and clean her eyelashes, separating each hair with the hook of its beak and licking with its pink slug of a tongue.

When my father got home from work, he and I would watch television and wait for dinner, tuna casserole or spaghetti with meat sauce, my mother taking a quick break from her online life to make the meal. On nights she ate with us on the couch, as soon as she finished her food, she'd move back upstairs to the office where the bird's cage lived next to the desk. My father called her hours at the computer *doing the dishes* because that's always where she was when he thought she should be doing the dishes. After dinner, my mother opened the birdcage door and offered the little stoop of her pointer finger like a sign-language X for the bird to take in its feet. They'd sit at the screen together, preening and posting, until their one- or two-AM bedtime, long after my father and I had fallen asleep.

My mother hated clipping the bird's wings; she didn't want to feel like its captor, like she was keeping it from doing what it was meant to. So, one day, she stopped and let the jagged flight feathers grow into their natural taper, and the bird started flying

10

free through the house. It became increasingly difficult to coax the bird down from curtain rods and light fixtures. We cleaned its shit off the rugs and mirrors and dining chairs we never sat in; we couldn't turn on the ceiling fans. Evenings into nights, though, my mother and the bird kept their usual routine, now with the office door closed.

On a weekday while I was at school, my mother opened the back screen door to pull some laundry from the line, and the bird flew out. We'd all been so careful at first to open the door just a crack enough for our bodies to pass through, keeping the bird in our sights all the while. Someone was bound to slip up eventually, but I never thought it would be her. When I got home, my mother was staring up the tree in the backyard where I could see the bird's slight yellow body hugging the trunk. We watched it, whistling and cooing its name, until dusk, and that night my mother sat alone at the computer. I don't remember if she cried.

The next morning, when the bird wasn't in the backyard, the two of us searched the block for the bright spot of yellow and found it in a towering oak a few houses up. There were other birds in the tree with it, and they were chirping. The bird stayed in the neighborhood a day or two longer, gradually flitting from one new home to the next and always further away from ours, until one day we took our morning walk to find the bird and didn't.

shitty father's day poem

did you know there's a species
of male fruit bat that lactates
so the female doesn't grow
too heavy with milk to fly,

or that flamingos agree on a nesting
site together and equally share
in their eggs' incubation time;

did you know my father left
a few days after I was cut into the world,
that my mother healed alone while he
was playing keeper at a soccer tournament,

or that my partner was held by his neck
up a wall as a child for being a child,
his father a handsome, devout, christian man.

the male midwife toad gestates
beneath the skin of his back legs,
and others carry offspring, instead,
in the wet of their mouths;

how hard it must be for the busy
new father not to swallow
his eager little tadpoles whole.

tree at the side of the road, and climbed up into the branches and hid there. The other was not so nimble as his companion, and could not escape, he threw himself on the ground and pretended to be dead. The Bear came up and snuffed all round him, he kept perfectly still and held his breath, for they say that a bear will not touch a dead body. The Bear took him for a corpse, and went whispered to him when he put his mouth to his ear. The other replied, "He told me never again to travel with a friend who deserts you at the first sign of danger."

Misfortune tests the sincerity of friendship.

Cat and Mouse in Partnership

The Brothers Grimm

As this story shows us, picking the wrong friend can be disappointing or even disastrous.

having made acquaintance with a mouse professed such great love and friendship for her, that the mouse at last agreed that they should live and keep house together.

little mouse, must not stir out, or you will be caught in a trap.

they took counsel together and bought a little pot of fat. And then they could not tell where to put it for safety, but after long consideration the cat said there could not be a better place than the church, for nobody would steal there, and they would put it under the altar and not touch it until they were really in want. So this was done, and the little pot placed in safety.

great wish to taste

"Listen to me, little mouse," said he, "I have been asked by my cousin to stand godfather to a little son. He is white partnership today, so let me go to it, and you stay at home and keep house."

"Oh yes, certainly," answered the mouse. "Pray go by all means. And when you are feasting on all the good things, think of me. I should so like a drop of the sweet red wine."

But there was not a word of truth in all this. The cat had no cousin and had not been asked to stand godfather. He went to the church, straight up to the little pot, and licked the honey off the top. Then he took a walk over the roofs of the town, saw his acquaintances, stretched himself in the sun, and licked his whiskers as often as he thought of the little pot of honey. And then, when it was evening he went home.

"So, you are at last," said the mouse. "I expect you have had a merry time."

"Well," answered the cat, "it went off very well."

"And what name did you give the child?" asked the mouse.

"Top-off," answered the cat dryly.

"Top-off!" cried the mouse. "That is a singular and wonderful name! Is it common in your family?"

"What does it matter?" said the cat. "It's not any worse than Crumb-picker, like your godchild."

A little time after this the cat was again seized with a longing.

"Again I must ask you," said he to the mouse, "to do me a favor, and keep house alone for a day. I have been asked a second time to stand godfather. And as the little one has a white ring around its neck, I cannot well refuse."

So the kind little mouse consented, and the cat crept along by the town wall until he reached the church, and going straight to the little pot of honey, devoured half of it.

"Nothing tastes so well as what one keeps to oneself," said he, feeling quite content with his day's work. When he reached home, the mouse asked what name had been given to the child.

"Half-gone," answered the cat.

"Half-gone!" cried the mouse. "I never heard such a name in my life! I'll bet it's not to be found in the calendar."

Soon after that the cat's mouth began to water again for the honey.

"Good things always come in threes," said he to the mouse. "Again I have been asked to stand godfather. The little one is quite black with white feet, and not any white hair on its body. Such a thing does not happen every day, so you will let me go, won't you?"

"Top-off, Half-gone," murmured the mouse. "They are such curious names, I cannot but wonder at them!"

"That's because you are always sitting at home," said the cat, "in your little gray frock and hairy tail, never seeing the world, and fancying all sorts of things."

So the mouse tidied up the house, and set it all in order. Meanwhile the greedy cat went and made an end of the little pot of honey.

"Now all is finished one's mind will be easy," said he, and home in the evening, quite sleek and comfortable. The mouse asked at once what name had been given to the third child.

"It won't please you any better than the others," answered the cat. "It is called All-gone."

"All-gone!" cried the mouse. "What an out-and-of-name! I never met with anything like it! All-gone! Whatever can it mean?" And shaking her head, she curled herself round and went to sleep. After that the cat was not again asked to stand godfather.

When the winter had come and there was nothing more to be had out of doors, the mouse began to think of their store.

"Come, cat," said she, "we will fetch our pot of honey, how good it will taste, to be sure!"

"Of course it will," said the cat.

So they set out, and when they reached the place, they found the pot, but it was standing empty.

"Oh, now I know what it all meant," cried the mouse, "now I see what sort of a partner you have been! Instead of standing godfather you have devoured it all, first Top-off, then Half-gone, then—"

"Will you hold your tongue!" screamed the cat. "Another word, and I'll devour you too!"

And the poor little mouse having "All-gone" on her tongue out it came, and the cat leaped after her and made an end of her. And that is the way of the world.

the bath

i	stood	in	the	bath
stood	in	the	bath	old
in	the	bath	old	enough
the	bath	old	enough	to
bath	old	enough	to	wash
old	enough	to	wash	myself
enough	to	wash	myself	my
to	wash	myself	my	mother
wash	myself	my	mother	shoved
myself	my	mother	shoved	a
my	mother	shoved	a	rag
mother	shoved	a	rag	between
shoved	a	rag	between	my
a	rag	between	my	legs
rag	between	my	legs	the
between	my	legs	the	soap
my	legs	the	soap	stung
legs	the	soap	stung	inside
the	soap	stung	inside	me
soap	stung	inside	me	and
stung	inside	me	and	i
inside	me	and	i	said
me	and	i	said	ow
and	i	said	ow	it
i	said	ow	it	hurts
said	ow	it	hurts	she
ow	it	hurts	she	said
it	hurts	she	said	no
hurts	she	said	no	it
she	said	no	it	doesn't
said	no	it	doesn't	
no	it	doesn't		
it	doesn't			
doesn't				

16

paige

when i was
a little girl,
i had a friend
named paige;
she was
the first time
i realized
a common
noun could
also be a
proper one.

i went home
with paige
and her mother
after school
once, and in
the car she
said her parents
were getting
a divorce.

in her room,
i asked if she
wanted to play
husband and

wife; she said
yes, and we
wedged our
small bodies
beneath the
bedframe
behind the
skirt and
rubbed
each other's
pubic bones
through cotton
underwear.

when we'd
finished and
crawled into
the daylight,
i told paige
that her father
didn't love
her anymore,
that she was
the reason
her parents
were getting
a divorce.

she cried
and told
her mother,
who got angry

and said it
was time for
me to leave;
on the drive
to my house,
just paige's
mother and
me, she asked
why i'd say
such a thing;
i'd never
even met
paige's father.

i remember
not knowing why
but feeling
so satisfied.

al pastor

i imagine
my body
as the lamb
gyro cone
spinning
behind the
counter of
my favorite
greek café
how easy
it would be
to flay apart
in chips
and strips
the seasoned
the sodden
the tender
meat of me

Flesh Creep

When my partner comes to bed, I tilt my phone to hide the screen. It's not porn or my ex's Instagram, not his ex's either. I'm not buying something we can't afford or swiping through Tinder under a different name. It's a video with a title in Arabic that Google translates to "Beauty is important, please join us." The thumbnail I clicked is presumably a still from the video itself, a closeup of a gloved finger pressed into rash-red skin—a cheek, maybe, or a chin. The pores around the fingertip are engorged, almost bursting, and serve as the backdrop for the centerpiece of the still: an opaque, brownish nodule of pus, oil, skin, and dirt speared by a needle like the last pickle in the jar.

Many of the acne-removal videos I watch are titled in languages I don't read—Vietnamese ("Bước số một. Hành trình thay đổi cho chàng trai trẻ," or "Step number one. Journey of change for the young man") and Thai ("Mụn Đầu Đen Gần Môi," or "Blackhead Near Lips"). Some are already translated for an English-language audience, like "Satisfying Relaxing with Sac Dep Spa" and "AWESOME FACIAL HIDDEN ACNE POPPING." At the beginning and end of the videos, sometimes we see the technicians, usually women, smiling behind disposable surgical masks, waving a quick hello or goodbye with one hand and bracing a lancet in the other. In some videos, the room is cramped and sparse, but others take place in an open area, like a lobby, with chairs lining the walls where people wait for their own services.

It's common that the viewer never sees the face of the client in its entirety, the camera zoomed in so tightly on a cluster of pores that the audience is relegated to one quadrant of the visage, or less, at a time, and I appreciate this. It's overwhelming to see so much of a person all at once in such a state of vulnerability, which, I suppose, is where my Venn diagram of zit-popping videos and porn overlap. I prefer to come watching only a mouth to a vulva and don't welcome the introduction of other parts. The disassociation both kinds of videos afford me personally is impossible to maintain when the bigger picture, the humanity, is in constant reveal. In this case, satisfaction is achieved by way of piecemeal consumption.

In high school, I spent swaths of the day at home in the bathroom, shirtless, popping pimples on my face and arms and chest until the skin and blood vessels beneath were broken and the areas were radiating red. My mother, too, spent hours on my back while I sat, hunched, in the shallow basin of the bathroom sink where the light was best, my forehead pressed against bent knees, with achy, pubescent breasts tucked behind forearms and elbows. It hurt; for hours, it hurt. I don't know the right language for it—obsession, compulsion, addiction, masochism, self-harm. I stopped wearing short-sleeve shirts and tank tops, the skin at my triceps perpetually splotched and sore, the scars on my back like a connect-the-dots puzzle or map of the stars. It tapered off at some point, I think when I moved into the dorms freshman year, unable to isolate for hours undisturbed and no good light anywhere anyway. With no one to work on my back, I took to scratching at the ones I could feel, my arm twisted up behind me in the shower or after dark in my extra-long twin. That's still how I do it.

Until the rise of *Dr. Pimple Popper*, I didn't know acne (cyst, limpoma, milia, ingrown hair, earwax, etc.) removal was a mainstream fixation. I thought it was niche, maybe even my own thing, in much the same way that, at age six, I thought I'd discovered masturbation (only to find out shortly thereafter from my mother that everyone does it, and it's a sin). I saw an episode of Dr. Lee's show on TLC once; it was playing on the flatscreen behind my nail technician during a manicure, and I was desperately uncomfortable at the public display of something I'd previously only enjoyed in private. (Is *enjoy* the right word?) Maybe it was a sensory clash of the moment—acetone and topcoat; the phantom sensation of the stubborn give and release between fortified fingernails; the sudden emergence of shit from just below the surface, the ombre ooze of a blackhead, spiraling.

Go

Loving you was finding the stall // in the food-court bathroom of the Battlefield // Mall with a toilet that wasn't already shit-stained // or floating a bloated tampon in a bowl of red wet //

two pale drops of piss I absorbed // off the peeling seat with a wad of single ply before // putting down a seat cover I never learned // to employ without compromising integrity //

You were an act of desperation // of holding the stall door closed with my foot // and trying not to breathe in // the overflow from the metal trashcan // loving you, if it had to be done, was fine

for a moment in time // it was fine

piecemeal

a rose by any other name would dissolve
in a jar of acid, could transition from one
state to another to no state ever again, to
nothing but something that was
just moments ago;

I was born breech, a blemish,
with my moon in the cancer
of a hospital bedsheet, in the early-
morning light of a slipping sun—

I was afraid of you; I'll say it
now:

I was afraid
            of you—

the bitter pill, swallowed, or was it
sweet, because the meat of me is
raw and wet and everything hurts
except coffee with cream, or whiskey
neat, and a Sausage McMuffin, a pill
so small it seems impossible strength
to stop the making, the feast.

Rot

My bottom molars are concave and pitted like the surface of the moon; they ache when I chew. I've been grinding my teeth since I was a child, and there's one tooth worse off than the rest, on my right side, with a crater the size of a raspberry seed. When one gets stuck from fresh fruit or jam, I can feel it, the small bit of resistance. Each seed beds down so deep that I almost feel bad excavating such a perfect fit with the nub of a bobby pin, tweezers or a pencil tip.

When I was a kid, a dentist told my mother I'd grow out of the grinding, but when I hadn't in a few years, she brought it up to a different dentist who suggested a nightguard we couldn't afford. Instead, my mother bought one of those boil-and-bite mouthguards for athletes; it was blue plastic and felt like hot tar against my gums when I bit for the impression. My mother held it out with a pair of tongs, and I wondered whether I should be putting something in my mouth that was too hot for her to hold

When we eventually found a dentist who made nightguards for cheap, the fit was off, so I spit it out in my sleep. In the morning, I'd pick it up off the floor, stuck with dog hair and carpet fibers. I stopped wearing it, and my mother stopped asking.

*

I don't go to the dentist as often as I should. I got sick of the gasps and tuts and same-old questions when I open to reveal cheeksful of ravaged enamel. Instead, for the past decade, I've been budgeting for Sensodyne and chewing food on the left side of my mouth, which, for some reason, is achieving a slower rate of deterioration. In the last year, though, I got my first job with benefits, and it seemed foolish not to take advantage of my plan after seeing how much I pay for it.

The hygienist asked questions I couldn't answer with her hands in my mouth, but before she tilted me back, I asked her not to gasp, and she didn't. When the dentist came, he said I needed a cap on my raspberry molar and then asked if I'm bulimic without ever actually saying the word.

"We rarely see this level of wear without there being *contributing factors.*"

I said my struggles were sporadic and long past, and he seemed satisfied.

"I trust you'd tell me," he said, "if this were an ongoing issue."

At my follow-up appointment, the receptionist ran my card for an amount just shy of that month's paycheck, and when it didn't decline, I was ushered to a chair with a soft blanket and a nitrous mask. During the procedure, the hygienist smeared balm on my lips when they went dry, and under the influence, I was sure I'd never been touched with such tenderness by another person; I thought the dentist, with his drill, might be etching his own miniature Mount Rushmore into what was left of my unfortunate tooth, a secret colonization.

They 3D-printed my new molar, or else a machine carved it from a ceramic cube. Either way, the hygienist held it up for me to see, and said it was what my tooth was always meant to look like. It was underwhelming, all convex and beefy, without any pits for seeds.

*

When it was fitted and sealed, the dentist told me it could be sensitive for up to a week and to be patient, but it's been two months, and I still can't chew on the right side of my mouth. Last week, on my way home from work, I tilted the rearview mirror down at a stoplight and dropped my jaw for a look. In the daylight, I could see a shock of black emerging beneath the opaque surface, like ink a glass of 2%.

Every day, the black gets blacker, the tooth still aches, and I'm still short a paycheck because I agreed to the handwritten deductible scrawled on a sheet of letterhead. And I know I need to call the receptionist, to tell her about the black and the ache so I can open up my mouth again for the people, so they can get it right this time. But every day, I drive past the storefront and keep on driving. Every day, I don't make the call.

a liberation

i.
a lime that is ripe
and left unpicked belongs to
the one who picks it

and when nobody picks the limes
from the alley tree of the ruined
house on tulip, i take them for myself;
ripeheavy, dim citrus breaks
the back of its elastic grace;
it begs

ii.
a palmetto bug
is a cockroach when it is
crawling in your bed

soft-white light through a window
at the rear, exposed bulb and pull string
above café curtains; either one person
or twelve live inside, and maybe once
a baby; pink highchair dirty plastic fisher
price on the porch, i make a bowl of my shirt
the first time, yes, the *first* time

iii.
do not forget to
draw a map back to your source
of rampant yielding

       across the street still on tulip
       a splinter of a house with a sign out front
       and no tenants just cicadas on the mailbox;
       everything overgrown, but the tree
       out front is fucking studded; it's hung
       as shit with pale pith, and maybe this
       is how it feels to be rich: too much to pick
       or, at least, too much to carry.

the weed

there's a weed i left to grow because
it wasn't in the way and that i let
keep growing in the periphery.

i thought it would be neat to see
if it could grow tall as me, and it did,
and then grew taller still.

it's almost to the roof of the house
now, with a strong trunk i can't
snap with one hand; i tried.

so, basically, it's a tree, with leaves
and branches and a network of roots;
to uproot it is to kill a constellation,

and what right do i have, anyway,
when i dared it grow taller
than me in the first place?

I'm here today, and

a strawberry didn't ripen to red, but one pinked up, finally, the first, and

the jalapeños are thick with pith and seeds, the darkest green I've seen in nature, and twining their stems from the mother trunk, woody at the base and strong enough for the delicate beginnings, cream-white as lace, to bring their centers to bear or yield to the breeze, a light touch from an impatient finger, down whence they sprung, and

the mint that survived the freeze, that announced itself green from a pile of dead and dying, from a fat patch of waste, has doubled itself again overnight and is growing new limbs up from the soil that snake from the pot and into adjacent ones, and

to touch a marigold is to smell like a marigold until my hands are washed and sometimes after, and

you can't let the basil go to seed, but don't ask me why when the rounded leaves start to grow in pointy you have to pinch them like a swollen tick, because the pointy leaves make way for the flowering, and the flowers turn to seed, and the basil can't go to seed because once it does the plant just stops and can't ever go back—there's no going back—but

don't ask me why.

It's the end of the world as we know it

While shopping what's left of the canned goods at the grocery store, an announcement at the top of the hour, robust and autotuned: "All employees must now perform a personal temperature check," and I, in a pair of disposable vinyl gloves but not a facemask because Dr. Gupta says they're unnecessary for the currently healthy, holding the last can of Kroger no-salt garbanzos, recall they've always made this announcement, but two weeks ago they were checking the temperature of the meats.

Distancing

My partner lost his job at the airport, in this Colorado mountain town of 6,500, because the last flight he worked for United had a single passenger. All the stores and restaurants are closed, all nonessential businesses, so he applied for a job at the hospital as a sanitizer; *They're desperate*, he said. Today, he was fitted for an N95 respirator mask, had three blood-draws, was pricked for TB; though, if the Senate bill passes, he'd likely make more on unemployment, *But that's not the point*, he says. *I want to look back on this time and know I helped people, that I was useful.*

I can see him from our living-room window, across the street at the food pantry where he volunteers on Wednesdays, bringing out prepackaged boxes for patrons, no one allowed inside the building now except for volunteers—Javier, Dusto, my partner, and a high schooler named Maria. Wednesdays are dedicated to the area's Spanish speakers, and he's been diligent about his Duolingo lessons. Every night I hear him in his office, *Sí, me gusta la ensalada de frutas*, followed by the trill that confirms a correct response.

At home, the tattoos on my hands are ashy and cracked because I wash them when I need to and when I don't. He brought me a mask, too, from the hospital, the disposable kind with the ear-loops. *You can wear it to the grocery store*, he says, sweetly, because he knows I'm already wearing vinyl gloves while I shop. Six years ago, I was diagnosed with hypochondria, and I'm still medicated for it, and other things, now. He always invites me to go with him to the pantry, and I'd planned to before the virus drove us all indoors. But he still goes, despite the risks, because he knows the odds are in our favor as late-20- and early-30-somethings. I know the statistics, too—we watch the news together—but they don't comfort me the way they do him, which I also know is part of my illness, the intimate understanding that I'm just as likely to be one of the unlucky few as the next 20-something. Maybe it's narcissistic, thinking I could always be the worst-case scenario, the exception rather than the rule.

I grew up delivering for Meals on Wheels with my mother, sitting in the back seat with stacks of Styrofoam clamshells that smelled like wet turkey stuffing and boiled brussels sprouts. When we were stationed in Altus, Oklahoma, we had a regular route and, on it, Mom's favorite delivery to a chatty old man named Clarence who lived in a trailer next to a tree on a dirt patch out in the country. I stayed in the car with the meals and watched from the window as she approached the doors of homes.

I was a nervous child, always, undiagnosed for what is clear to both of us now—OCD, general anxiety, the seeds of depression like she's struggled with, too, since childhood. I don't know what I expected to happen when people opened their doors to her, reaching for the slippery, lukewarm containers, but I always expected it. Occasionally, they'd ask her to come inside and carry the meals to the kitchen, and when my mother disappeared through the doorway, I held my breath until I could see her again. She'd walk back to the car, lock the doors with us inside, and head for the next stop, but I wished we could stay in the in-between, just the two of us, together, alone.

I understand my partner's impulse to help rather than to take, to use the privilege of our age and uncompromised immune systems for the good of others. I understand it because I grew up with it, and part of my mother's heart lives in me, beating right alongside my own; my partner learned it from his mother, too. But most of me wants to beg him, every day, not to leave, to lock our door to the world until it's safe again to stand within six feet of another human; to keep washing my hands and watch the seasons change from the windows while the government pays our rent. Most of me wants to exist as an island with the person I love, healthy in our little bubble, listening only to the one heart and not the imploring second, just the two of us, together, alone.

when the job you worked your ass off for is given to an older white man with a soul patch, you ask your partner to fuck you with the lights on

and he obliges, because he loves you and also loves
fucking you // he's good at it, but even still, you
have to try not to think about campus visits and
job talks // about the novel you haven't worked on
in months // about the ten pounds you've gained
(at least) since taking this job in the first place,
since moving to a valley in Colorado, between
mountain ranges you don't love the way everyone
else does, mountains that only ever looked like
piles of cash, too rich for your blood, thicker at
7,000 feet // about the young men in your lit class
who say Harjo is whiny and Bechdel is boring and
that Octavia Butler really *was* writing about slavery
when she says she wasn't writing about slavery,
who tell you they wouldn't have taken your class if
they'd known how *depressing* it would be, learning
what it means to live as a woman in their world
// but they'll like the new guy, or else won't give
him much trouble, because he looks like what a
professor *should* look like—lanky, glasses, balding,
shirt & tie // and you guess he's probably never
had a student flirt with him in a free-write or try
to talk to him about *girl problems* during office

hours // probably not // and you know you won't come with your partner fucking you like this, and he knows it too, but he also knows you're hurt and angry and that this is the first time you're not crying in days, and because you know he won't stop fucking you until you tell him to, grab the vibrator off the nightstand and close your eyes.

Cape Fair

There is a house on an acre of land in Southwest Missouri, that was built by three Amish men and their sons. My grandfather is dying there, now—has decided to die by concentration of ammonia in his blood, of liver disease.

His brothers have traveled with their wives from Texas and Florida, his eldest daughter from Arkansas, and his youngest, a son, from Southern California. My mother is the middle child, always her father's favorite—bookish and quiet. She's the child he never had to worry about, the one who lives nearby and knows to make the coffee so weak you can see to the bottom of a full mug, just how he likes it.

When I was a child, I loved my grandfather with an awkward desperation; I'd do anything for his attention but could sense I wore on his nerves. Sometimes during our visits, he'd let me sit in his den and watch low-budget horror and sci-fi movies while he worked on his stamp collection, but I asked too many questions and touched things I wasn't supposed to, left fingerprints on the glass of his Navy shadowboxes and replica submarines. He did love me then, though, when I attended Sunday school and helped my grandmother brown hamburger for tostadas, when I begged to read the poems he wrote and kept in his desk drawer, with their ABAB rhyme schemes, handwritten on notebook paper. The family has always been so proud of his poetry.

I don't know when he stopped loving me, only the moment I understood he didn't anymore, or that some sort of bad outweighed whatever good he still felt toward me. I was 16, and my mother and I were living with her parents for the summer while my father was on his last deployment to the Middle East. She and I attended the First Baptist Church of Cape Fair where my grandfather served as a deacon, or still does. Though, I assume it's more of an honorary title now that he can't walk stairs or count his own dice during Yahtzee.

It was during youth group in the basement while the adults were upstairs for Wednesday-night service—my grandmother in the nursery, my grandfather ushering the collection plate, my mother sitting alone in a pew. I was talking to the pastor's son, the only other high schooler I knew, trying to impress him with parroted information about local fishing prospects:

"My grandpa's the one who taught me how to clean a fish. Last week, I asked if he'd take me fishing on Table Rock, but he says the Lake is way too high right now, so I guess we have to wait."

The pastor's son looked confused, shook his head, and said, "Yeah, that's not really the way it works. Fishing's better when the Lake is up. And anyway, your grandpa went fishing with my dad a couple days ago. Not sure why he told you that."

My grandfather took me fishing for the first time when I was eight. Mom, Dad, and I had driven from Altus Air Force Base, Oklahoma, to the San Diego suburb where my grandparents lived for 25 years before settling in rural Missouri. Their two-bedroom in Santee barely fit the dozen of us who showed for the holidays every other year. There was a front-porch swing and a white couch I wasn't allowed to sit on except for Christmas morning. The centerpiece of the back patio was an enormous shell chandelier my mom brought back from her time stationed in the Philippines, and the entire house, especially the towels, smelled like my grandmother's perfume.

I always knew love in that house, but I was easier to love then. I was compliant when I was a kid, too afraid of testing the waters. I do wonder, though, when my grandfather realized I wouldn't always be so easy, that one day his age and our shared DNA wouldn't be enough to warrant my respect or admiration without effort. Only sometimes do I wish I had tried harder to keep being the granddaughter he could love—a woman of god, servant of men, bearer of children, and holder of my tongue; a woman who gives her respect before asking it in return.

My mother called me one night a few months ago to check in, but mostly, I think, to tell me that her father, a Type 2 diabetic, was in the hospital after he snuck a bag of marshmallows from the pantry while nobody was watching and ate them, one by one, until the plastic was empty. This was before he quit his treatments and medications, before everyone understood that he's dying on purpose.

The doctors have been cautioning his weight for a decade, but he refuses to diet; my grandmother has tried. I always knew him with a bit of a belly. He's Italian, and my grandmother is Mexican, so we ate big meals—pans of lasagna and platters of red rice—but when they lived on the West Coast, he went out several nights a week to metal detect the beaches. I remember his calves so strong they looked like skin stretched over softballs from hours of walking through sand. These days, though, he has trouble getting from room to room, and the only clothes he wears are a pair of bib overalls.

When I was a teenager, my mother told me how she and her

father would stay up later than the rest of the family, would drink coffee together in the middle of the night at the kitchenette. She said he wasn't always so conservative, that he admitted to her during those late-night talks that he wasn't sold on absolutes or capital-T truths, and I think she held on to that version of her father in the decades that followed.

My mother is a woman who is all in until she's out, devout until she's apostate, in every regard except her family. She seems a bottomless well of compassion and understanding in the face of being silenced, criticized, ignored, and taken advantage of by those she loves. There has to be a word for it: the rage and indignation felt on behalf of a person who does not feel it for themselves. As a woman in her 50s, my mother is watching her father die in real-time, having her last coherent moments with him. I think she expected wisdom and perspective, moments from their 1980s kitchenette before she loses him for good. Instead, she's found herself risking vulnerability with the dogmatic grandfather I grew up with rather than the uncertain father she did, a man who was fucked up and absent and sometimes cruel but who was real when she needed him to be.

I'm not sad my grandfather is dying, and I won't make the trip to Cape Fair to say goodbye. We never did have much to say to each other, and anymore I have as little interest in reading his poetry as he has in reading mine. I've heard it's lucky, the easy way I have of cutting ties and moving on with life, of letting go. But sometimes it makes me feel broken, like I'm missing something inherently human that I don't think of blood the way others seem to or feel beholden to people for existing so I could exist too.

There's a line from Toni Morrison's *Beloved*, when Sethe says, "Love is or it ain't. Thin love ain't love at all," and every time

I read it, I know it bone deep. I have no interest in a love that is not specific to me, that is not rich and full and without condition; I have no interest in love out of obligation or familiarity, because it's too easy. Blood is too easy a reason for love.

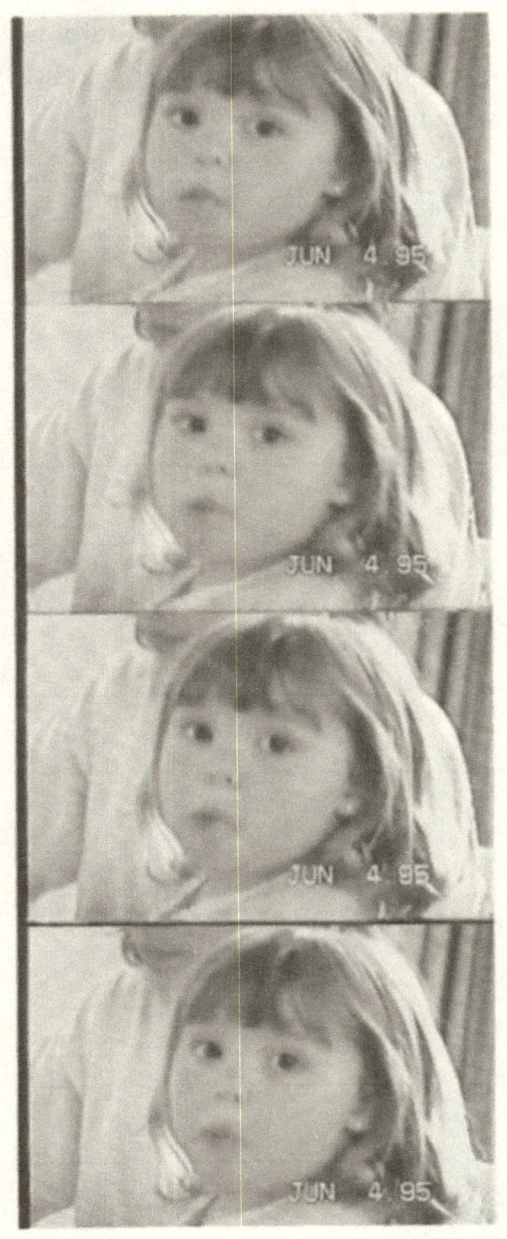

Unbrained

44

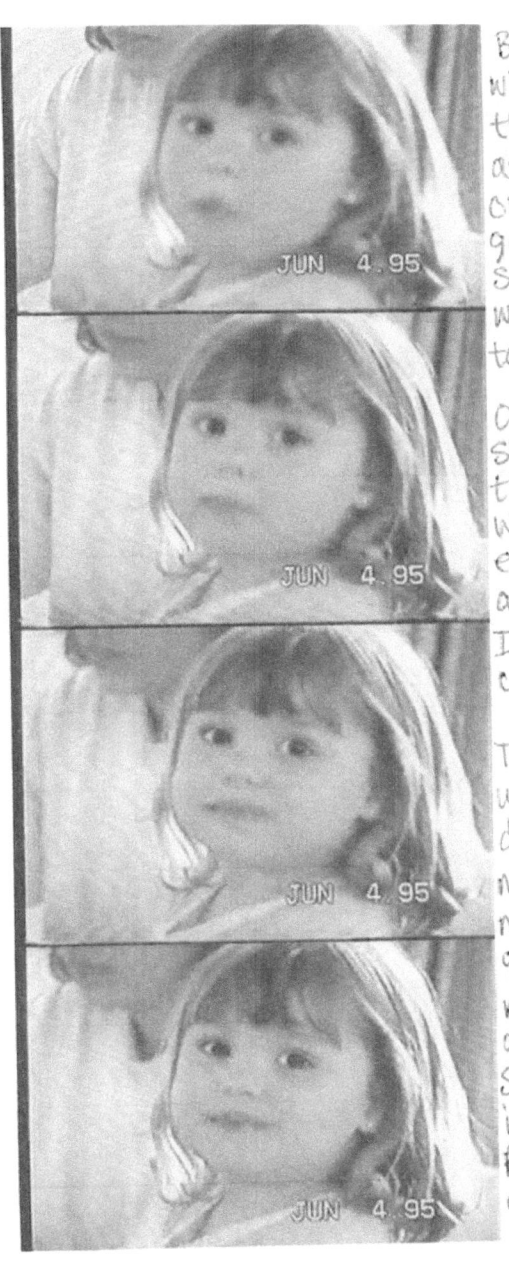

Before diagnosing me with bipolar depression, the psychiatric nurse asked me questions for over an hour and then gave me a mood-disorder survey on a clipboard with a pen attached by tape and yarn.

One of the questions she asked about midway through the appointment was whether I'd experienced any childhood abuse, and I said what I always do: not that I can recall.

This means no to most who ask, and the nurse didn't hesitate in marking my answer and moving onto the next question. But a few minutes later, she asked about my childhood, something general, like if I was a happy kid. And I stalled out; I always stall out. I don't know how to say it.

Last year, my mother had some of our home videos converted to digital files and sent them to me. They're mostly holidays my ages two and three. In one, it's Christmastime, and I'm in a tartan dress with a lace collar, playing a kiddie keyboard for my mother's parents we're visiting in San Diego. We're in the all-white living room no one's allowed in except for special occasions.

In another video, it's my birthday, and we're in our little enlisted house on McClellan, an Air Force base in Sacramento that closed in 2001. I'm cherubic, with plump cheeks and a round, protruding belly; I speak breathlessly, tearing open gifts and stripping without regard for the camera to try on my new

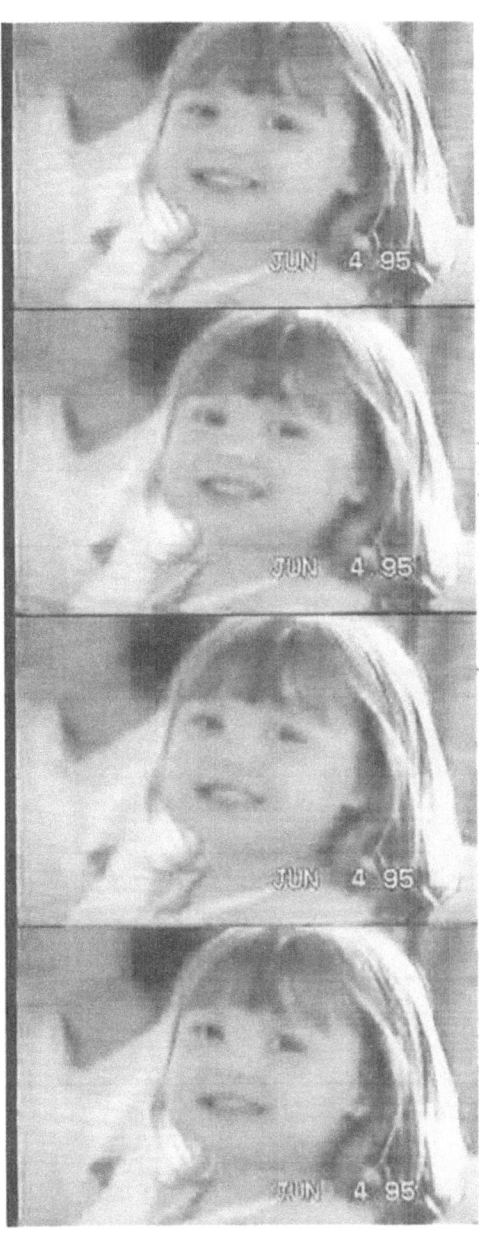

matching top-and-bottoms set straight from the wrapping paper. At the table, I proffer generous, frosting-heavy lumps of cake to my waiting mouth. Chockfull of baby teeth. It's just my parents and me.

From the first time I went to open one of the files, I was nervous, and I've been nervous every time since. I have no good reason for it. I had a happy enough childhood. I smiled for photos and socialized with other kids, and aside from various deployments, I had both my parents.

But the strange thing is, I don't remember much from birth to adolescence; my childhood is a haze. It shocks my mother often, all that I can't recall— honestly, I think it hurts her.

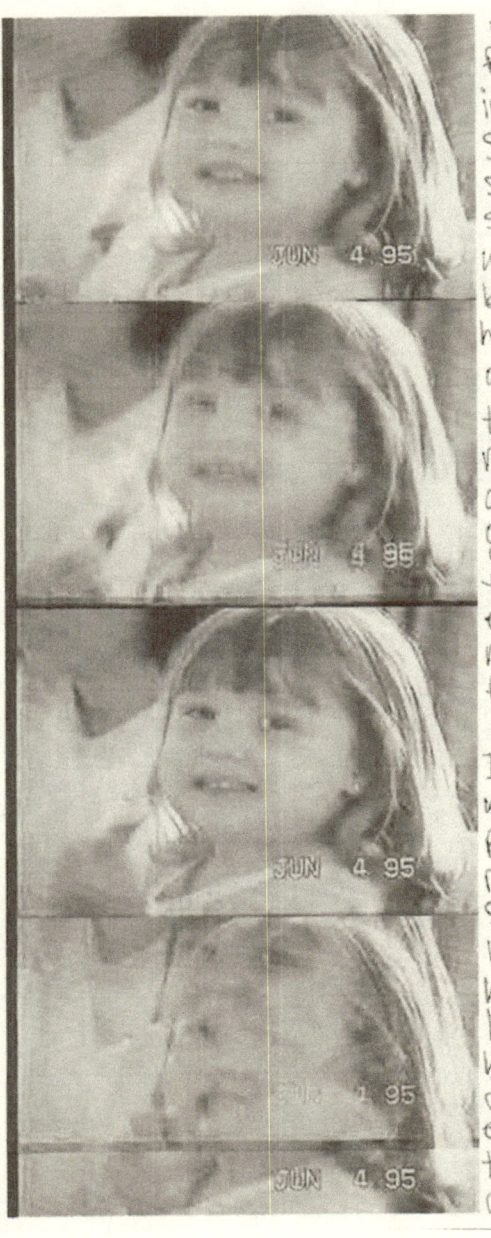

When I opened that first file, though, Christmas in the early nineties in Southern California, I started sobbing at the sight of myself. I was watching alone in the bedroom, my husband on his computer in the adjacent office. I kept the volume low and cried noiselessly in a gutteral ache, my wet mouth gaping. I watched until the pressure behind my eyes grew so it felt they might bulge to burst and turned it off.

It isn't like me to hide my sorrow from my partner, but this reaction was a total surprise. When we watch his home videos, we coo sweetly over his baby and toddler selves; he offers additional details and context for each scene, and every time his mother, who died the year before we met,

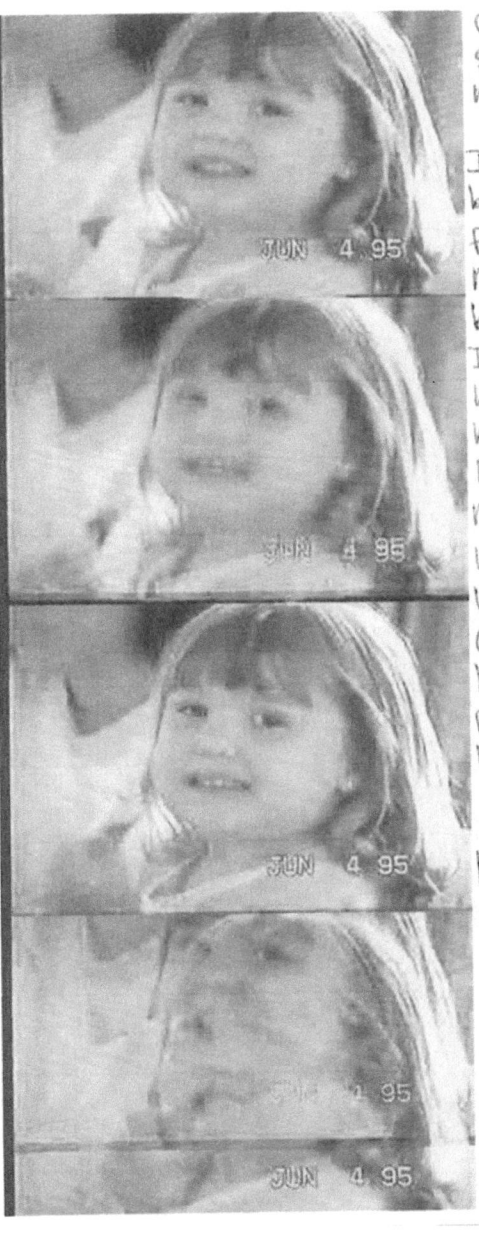

comes on screen, he smiles. The footage makes him happy.

I waited almost a year before trying another file from the batch my mother sent, the birthday video. This time, I invited my husband to watch with me, thinking maybe I was in the wrong headspace all those months ago, that maybe watching my videos the way we watched his, cuddled up together in bed, might promote the reaction I expected and hoped for.

But the same thing happened at the sight of my three-year-old self: I started weeping and couldn't stop. Eventually, we had to pause, and after his t-shirt was thoroughly saturated at the chest, I said, "I don't know what's

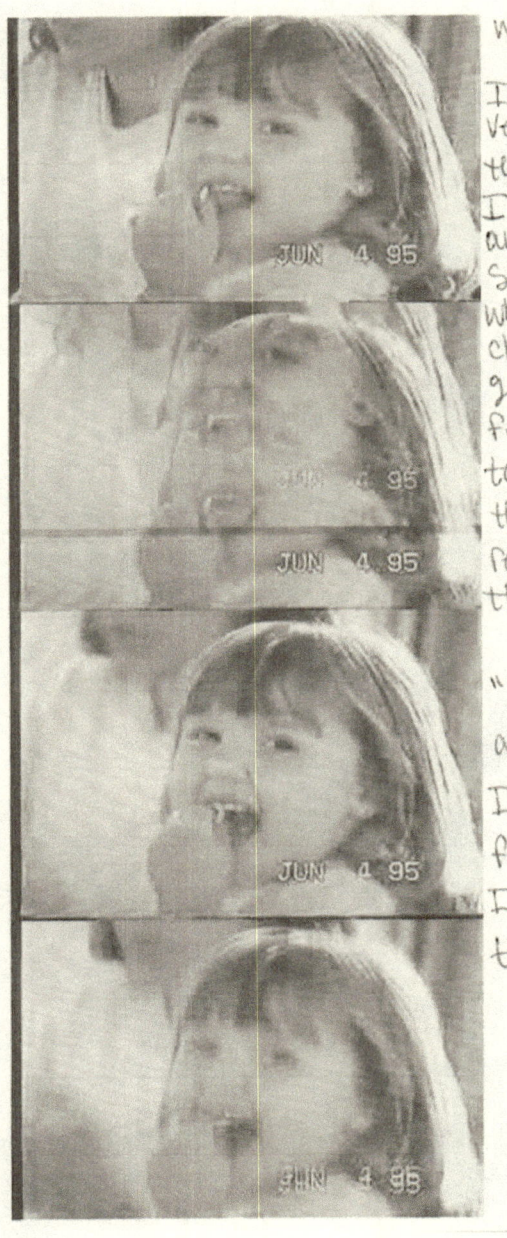

wrong with me."

I attempted a briefer version of all this for the psychiatric nurse. I told her I don't recall any childhood abuse or serious trauma but that when I think of my childhood, I'm sad and get a knot in my gut; I feel shame and an almost total disassociation from that self. I struggle to recall ever existing in that body.

"I don't remember anything happening," I told her, "but I feel like it did. And I don't know what to make of that."

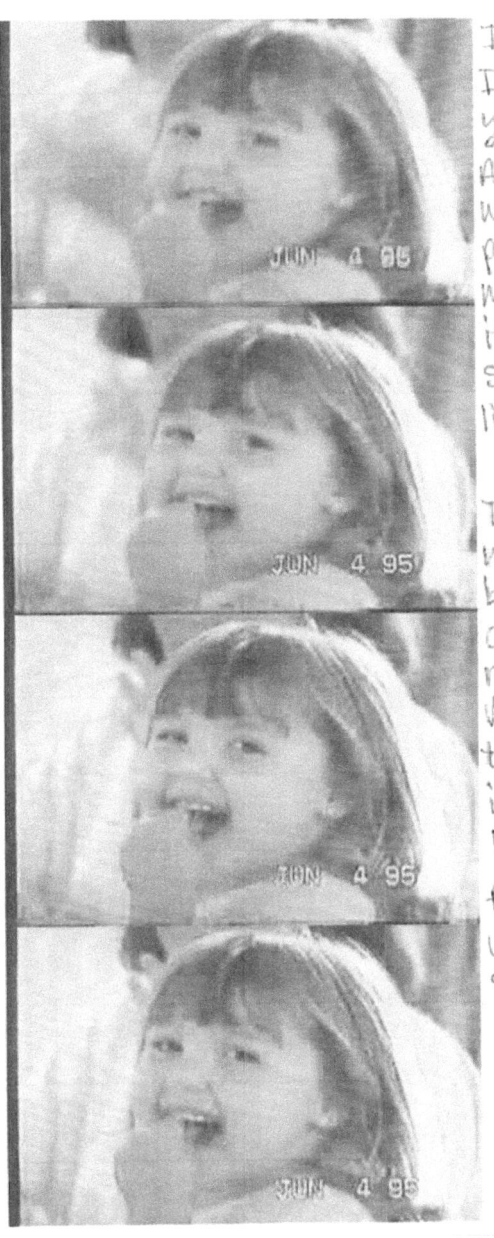

It was the first time I'd verbalized it after years of a silent knowing. And what's more, the woman, a psychiatric professional, validated me. She said, "Whatever it is — and it is likely something — it sounds like you've repressed it."

That was all. We kept on with our questions because unearthing childhood traumas was not the purpose of the visit, but I'd said the thing, and she heard it. She said probably Yes, and suddenly it felt like part of me was allowed to make sense.

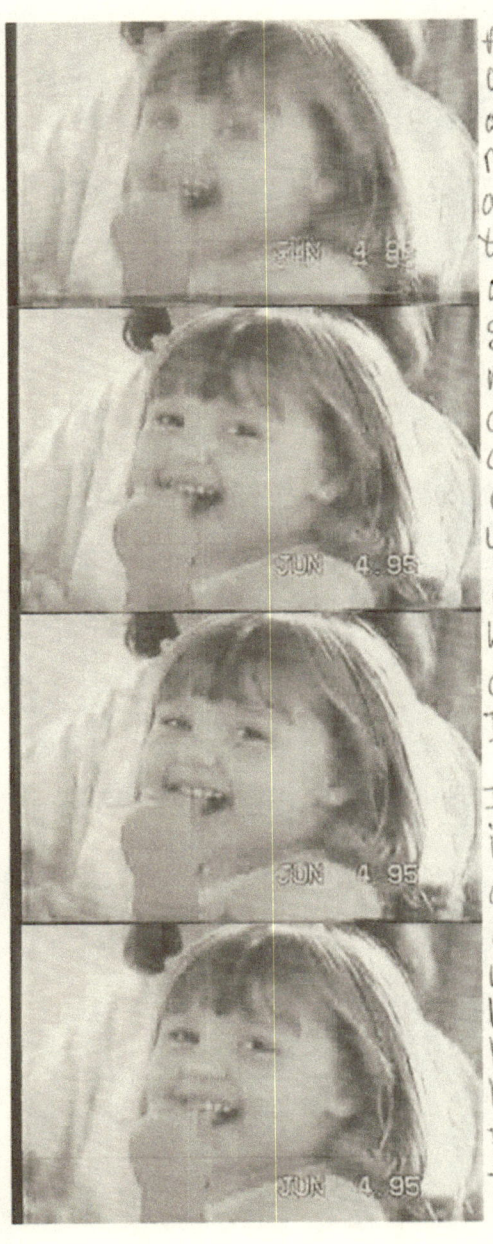

At the end of the appointment, after my answers and survey results added up to her anticipated diagnosis — though, one I hadn't anticipated for myself — She prescribed a medication I'd seen cheesy pharmaceutical commercials for on cable tv, one that, if you google it, is listed as an antipsychotic, which elicits in me a different kind of shame I have to fight.

I don't know yet that it's the right dosage or medication or diagnosis even; to be mentally ill is to always have a follow-up on the books. It's hard to know I'm what some people call crazy, that to nurses and doctors

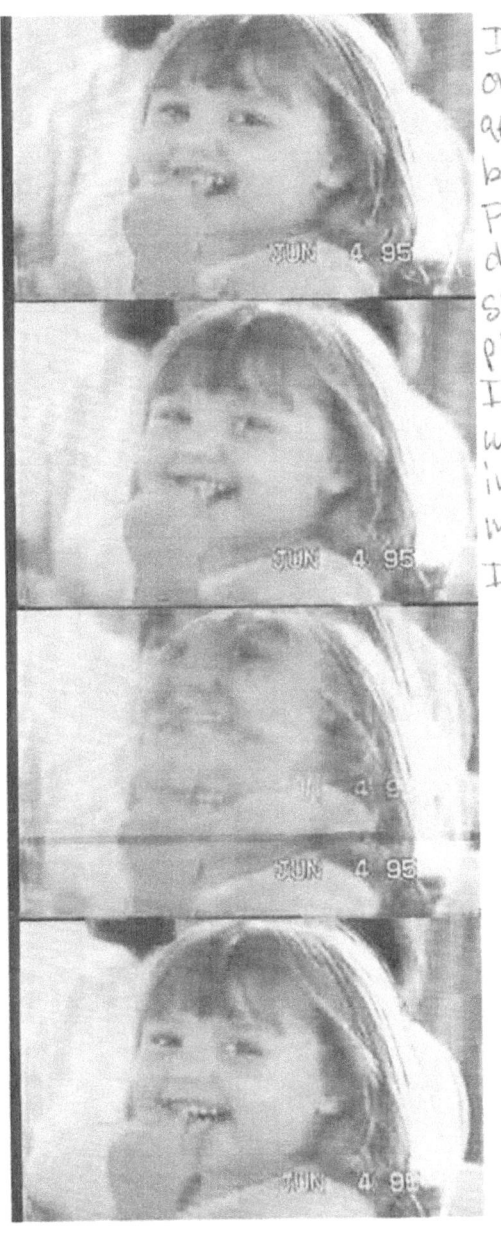

I'm one to keep an eye on. And until this appointment, I'd never been told by a medical professional that my deepest knowing, the shit that bubbles in the pits of me, is something I can trust, that even when I can't conjure image or language to match what I ~~feel~~, I can still call it truth

i left your blood on my ankle
for a few minutes longer
than i had to after you'd gone

i let it dry to brown
before washing it
with ivory in the tub

your head in my lap
i felt fear by osmosis
and you felt the fleece
of my housecoat my
hand on your chest

i hadn't even seen
that you were bleeding
until they took you away

dew claw

i found my dog's dew claw under my pillow like a lost baby tooth; beneath the claw is a raw, pink nub, a little clit, that glistens slick until it starts to gather dust, it forms a crust, and eventually the dog loses interest, takes off the cone of shame that kept her from tasting the metallic sweetness, velvet pain, of her domesticated body.

Thick Like Me

On a campus shuttle my sophomore year of undergrad, a woman sat next to me and whined about her beet-red sunburn. I was polite and smiled and listened about her weekend at the lake.

"You'd understand if you were white," she said, and my stomach seized up. I'm mixed, but it'd been a while since anyone called it out like that. I'd forgotten that when white people say that shit, it feels like an accusation; it feels like being caught.

*

My partner thinks astrology is bullshit, but if you ask me, I'm a Gemini sun, Cancer moon, and Leo rising. I'm also an INFP-T, an Enneagram 4w3, and my love language is words of affirmation; though, I tend to show love by giving gifts. According to my Enneagram results, I'm a compulsive identity seeker, and it's embarrassing to admit I needed the test to tell me as much.

I don't see myself clearly; I never have. I'm fighting a lifelong battle against dysmorphias of body, intellect, and achievement. And a few years ago, in my mid-twenties, I realized I've also been enduring a crisis of heritage, of blood. As a young person who felt the inescapable friction of never quite fitting into the homogenous society and culture in which she was raised, I thought the only way I might ever stand out as worthy of affection and admiration and love was to blend in at all costs. And because of this thinking, I rebuffed any threat to the veneer of whiteness, even the ones I now see as rife with potential offerings.

*

I attended middle school at Bethel Baptist in Hampton, Virginia. It was a K-12 school and most of the classes were taught by people without education degrees, who may not have had degrees at all; I doubt the school was accredited. Most of the teachers were parents, as were the "librarians." We read a lot of Jane Austen, memorized carefully selected poems from Dickinson and Longfellow and Frost. Each book in our closet of a library was hand-selected and approved by a committee comprised of the very same parents and teachers and church elders. We had chapel every school day and were expected to attend the adjacent Baptist church with our families on Sundays. We also had a mandatory retreat at a rural camp every year, which all the students plus chaperones travelled to by bus.

One evening on the retreat, I was changing at my bunk before dinner, and Tiffany, a Black girl in my class, looked over at me in my underwear, and said, "Dang, girl, I thought you were skinny like all these other white girls, but you're thick like me."

I don't remember how I responded—though, I probably let out a nervous giggle and ran to hide in a bathroom stall—but I do remember obsessing over the comment and feeling deeply conflicted for a long time after. I was moved that another person had recognized themselves in me, had named a thing that made us like, which my white friends never did. But I was afraid and ashamed that what she recognized of me didn't conform to what I understood was beautiful: thinness and whiteness. And I didn't know how to locate value in any part of me that was anything else.

*

Sometimes my mother texts me pictures of photographs of Mexican relatives I've never met. My great-grandmother, Alice Salazar, had five children and refused to teach them Spanish. This was a rare detail about my grandmother's childhood and something I couldn't understand when she said it while chopping cucumber for Sunday lunch's obligatory iceberg side salad. When I asked why, she said she didn't know but that her mother only wanted her kids to speak English.

In 2019, I met an art professor named Mariella while teaching at a university on Colorado's Western Slope. We were the faculty advisors for the two components, visual art and literature, of the campus literary magazine. We actually liked each other, so our advisor meetings took place at a brewery over snacks and beers, and I learned she's from Puerto Rico. Mariella and her husband had brought her mother from Puerto Rico to live with their family in Colorado, and they'd hoped to bring her brother and his family too after Hurricane Maria, but the Trump administration had squashed that dream for the time being.

Eventually, I told Mariella about my Mexican heritage and how I'd only really learned about it once I was grown. I told her my grandmother never spoke Spanish because her mother refused to teach it, and that any culture Alice may have known had stopped with her. I told her when my grandmother was 15, she married my grandfather, a Navy submariner, and that now they're Southern Baptist Conservatives retired in rural Missouri. They love ranch dressing and Sean Hannity and don't own a spice rack, and we rarely talk about the people and places we come from.

Mariella said she wasn't surprised, that from what she understood, it's fairly common for Latinx immigrants, especially from Mexico, and first-generation US citizens not to pass on their native languages as a matter of survival. It's seen as a burden to bear, just one more thing to render them other. And so, culture is lost; histories are erased; blood is bleached.

*

When I say I didn't know about my Mexican heritage until I was older, that's not to say I didn't know I was different where I grew up. I was raised on bases across the US and in England, where I was born and where my dad is originally from. Military bases are white places. We knew a little more diversity in our neighborhoods because my father was enlisted, not an officer, meaning he joined up without first getting a college degree. The officers' neighborhoods were almost exclusively white, with bigger, newer houses and nicer lawns; they had separate clubs and facilities. Lots of officers, too, chose to live off-base where they could maintain a higher standard of living, and their families often got to stay longer in one place.

When I was eleven, we were stationed in Altus, Oklahoma, and my best friend, Ashley, was the daughter of a base dentist, an officer. There was a creek that split base housing into two sides; on one, the enlisted side, all the streets were named after flowers (we were on Honeysuckle), and on the other, the officers' side, they were named for trees. There's a photo from my eleventh birthday in an album in the upstairs closet of my parents' house in Southwest Missouri where they retired to be near my grandparents. I'm an only child, and my mother hates parties and socializing, so for birthdays I was allowed to pick one friend to spend the day with. That year, we went to a minor-league baseball game and a sit-down restaurant for dinner. I picked Ashley, and before we left for the game, my mom took us to the Base Exchange to buy matching dresses. They were early-2000s glam, the discount version of something worn by an Olsen twin—ombréd green and yellow lycra with curled hems. Ashley's size small hung loose from her slight, athletic frame; she wasn't wearing a bra yet and didn't need to. Everything about her was long—her milk-white, freckled face; her straight, blonde hair; her arms and legs and torso.

In the photo, Ashley and I are sitting in the stands of the small stadium, looking back over our shoulders and smiling with teeth. These were the preteen years before makeup and cell phones, when I insisted on carrying a purse even though the only things I had to put in it were Lip Smackers and a velcro wallet with my military ID. We're sweaty and happy, and the Oklahoma sun is beating down; the tops of Ashley's cheeks and nose have started to burn red, and next to her, there I am: a deep, bronze tan, my brown hair parted down the middle and accentuating the roundness of my face and fulness of my cheeks. I look like a little Latina. Seeing the photo now and knowing that's how I looked to everyone around me, it makes sense why I felt different: in the whitewashed, militaristic spaces I grew up in, uniformity was expected, and I am essentially varied.

*

My father is white, with light brown hair that turns blonde in the sun and small, blue eyes; his pale body is covered in freckles. When he'd show up for school events, smelling of Faultless heavy starch and Kiwi shoe polish in his camouflage uniform, kids would ask if he's my "real" dad. The spitting image of my mother, no one has ever questioned whether I'm hers. My mother bears a strong resemblance to her own mother too, but as a military kid without enduring family ties, I never really gave much thought to who came before my mother's mother.

Both my parents grew up poor, and their parents grew up poorer. I can't trace my lineage back on either side past my great-great-grandparents, people I'd have almost been able to meet during my lifetime. What I know of my ancestors is mostly missing census data, dashes and blank spaces on government forms; it's a lack of photographic evidence of their existence. It's relying on my grandmother's failing (and repressed) memory for details to help piece together who and where I'm from. It's the understanding that addiction, incarceration, and abuse are rampant factors discussed euphemistically and often glossed over entirely; it's my grandmother whispering to my mother about *bad men*.

When I search my Mexican family name, Salazar, for the first time, I learn how incredibly common it is and that it will be of no help in uncovering anything about my heritage. I also learn that housekeeping is a common occupation for Salazars. Throughout my mother's childhood, while her father was out to sea, her mother held jobs as a hotel maid. When I was in high school, after 15 years as a homemaker, my mother, too, took a job with a maid service and worked as part of a cleaning crew. Both women are neat and orderly; though, my mother's standards (and my father's) are so high, she calls herself a mess.

I took a job as a housekeeper once, when I was a freshman in college. My mother was working at a retirement home, and an elderly woman said her son was looking for a cleaner. I was broke, so my mother suggested me. He left a key under the doormat, a caddy of cleaning supplies, and a check for $50 on the banquet inside. I had no idea what the fuck I was doing. After accepting the job, I'd googled "how to clean like a professional" because at 18 I was too stubborn to ask my mother for advice. I didn't know to squeegee water droplets from the shower doors or that I was supposed to wipe off the residue left by the granite cleaner once it dried. I tried to leave a light-dark checker pattern in the carpet with the vacuum like it said to online, but it looked easier when the woman on YouTube did it.

That night, as I ate in the campus dining hall, I got a call from the man whose house I'd cleaned. He laughed at me over the phone, pausing at one point as though I might explain myself, but for which infraction, exactly, I wasn't sure, so I stayed quiet. Eventually, he said I could keep the check, but my services wouldn't be required again. I said okay and hung up before the man could tell me just how useless I was—before I started to cry.

*

My freshman and sophomore years of high school we were stationed on a base in Alaska. I took photos at school events for the yearbook with the film camera I bought on eBay, and one winter, the editor assigned me to the Snowball Dance, which I hadn't planned on attending because nobody asked. I wore something sparkly and watched couples dance all evening through the viewfinder, but the only attention I got was from José, a Mexican guy a year above me. He asked me to dance a few times, but I always feigned preoccupation with the picture taking, and none of the white girls would dance with him, so he wallflowered most of the night.

I'd pop out of the dance occasionally to hang out with a couple fellow yearbook staffers who had volunteered to take tickets and nominations for Snowball King and Queen outside the gym. One guy said he noticed José had been hovering around me all night and asked why I didn't dance with him.

"You don't have to take pictures *all* night," he said, but I told him I wasn't interested in José, that I didn't want to dance with him.

I went back inside just before they announced Snowball royalty, and I was poised to take a picture of the winners when the announcer said José's name and mine. Apparently, no votes had been cast for the award—it was 40-below outside, and the dance had been sparsely attended—so the yearbook staff put our names in the shoebox because they wanted José to have his dance and thought we were cute together. Someone put a fuzzy, pink tiara on my head and gave José a plastic scepter, and everyone cleared the floor to watch us dance to Chris Brown's "With You."

José's smile was wide, and he sang every word to the song with both hands at my waist. He tried to maintain eye contact, but I couldn't hold his gaze, breaking every few seconds. My face was hot; people were staring and whispering around us, and I was desperate to know what they were saying about us, about me. I remember being awed, too, though, by José's openness. He was so happy to be dancing with me. I was deeply uncomfortable at being wanted by another person and had no idea how to receive his desire. Instead, I wanted to disappear.

I've thought about that dance hundreds of times in the fifteen years since. I've wondered why I didn't just dance with José when he asked in the first place. I was always pining to be asked to do anything. The truth is I didn't want to dance with José because none of the white girls would, and if I did, that made me different from them. So, when I was finally dancing with José and racked with embarrassment, it wasn't because I didn't like the person I was dancing with—he was sweet and kind and cute—it was because I was wondering why they'd chosen me to be his queen.

*

My mother's understanding of her Mexican heritage was steeped in stereotype when I was growing up. She told me I had "child-bearing" hips long before she could have known what shape they'd take and said people with our skin tone should never wear yellow. Sometimes she called me "chica," but it was only one of three or four words she knew in Spanish, and she carries a deep shame at her lack of interest in cooking and her hatred of cilantro.

I've always known my mother as an identity seeker too; though, I didn't realize that's what she was doing until I was older. We jumped from church to church on her whim, and I went back and forth between the base school and church school and homeschool throughout my childhood and adolescence. She was always on a different diet, buying special books and pills and powders for them online. She still cycles through phases with religions and politics and projects. A few years ago, she asked me to attend the mass where she'd become an official member of the Catholic Church after a year of devoutness and RCIA classes. I went home with my parents for dinner after the ceremony, and my mother confided she was thinking of "doing a year without god" and had been watching talks by atheists online.

For most of my life, I hated how unreliable my mother was. How she could go from a movie lover one day to having me smash any of our VHS tapes rated PG or higher in the driveway with a hammer; from telling me my virginity was something sacred, my body meant for my husband alone, to giving me blowjob lessons in the kitchen of our apartment at 16. It was a confusing and turbulent way to grow up, but as I've gotten older, I've realized my mother has always been just as desperate for identity as I am; she just has other people depending on her for shit while she tries to figure herself out. I've always kept people at a distance and still do. Today, I don't have close friends, I don't want kids, and I've severed numerous family ties for safety and political reasons. My partner and I married ourselves without witnesses on a park bench in Colorado, which is, apparently, legal in the Centennial State. But it's hard to share yourself with someone, anyone, when you're not sure who exactly that self is, when even the simplest shit, like who and where you're from, is in constant negotiation.

*

I had a good friend in adulthood once, our relationship spanning five or six years—my longest to date. She was mixed too, her mother Mexican and her father white, and every time we went out together, we were mistaken for sisters. When we lived in the same city, we'd go out for tacos and take shots of tequila and tan by the pool. She wasn't fluent in Spanish but grew up with her mother speaking it and visiting their family in Mexico. She loved to talk to me about her mother, a real matriarch—a fierce, loyal, hard-working woman who once fed a street dog meat and glass after it tried to bite my friend when she was little girl.

"You don't fuck with my mother," she'd say.

When I moved to start my MFA in Michigan, she moved to Portland, Oregon because she'd always wanted to. She started a ceramic-jewelry business, and I'd order earrings in wacky shapes and bright colors to support her early on. We started growing apart but made an effort to keep in touch. We talked on the phone a few times, and she'd send me little notes with the earrings I ordered. In one, she dreamed up a trip for the two of us to Mexico since I'd never been. She said we'd get in touch with our ancestors and learn more about ourselves and each other. She's always been the best dreamer. In one package, she sent a stick of Palo Santo that I still have and burn when I know the moment's right. I was living alone in the Upper Peninsula, pursuing writing hundreds of miles from anyone I knew. She was hustling in Portland, waiting tables and making art. And we had this plan together, two Mexican girls, seeking.

When the AWP conference was in Portland, I slept on her couch. We were seeing each other for the first time in years, and things were a little awkward. We hadn't talked for months before I messaged to ask if I could stay with her, but I was still excited and kept the dream of our Mexico trip alive and tucked away. I wanted to see her favorite places in the city, to shop vintage, eat and drink, and talk about life. But there was an instant formality when I arrived, a brusqueness about her that I couldn't pin down. I attended my conference, and she worked her shifts, and we carved out one whole day to spend together, just us. That morning, we stopped first at the post office, and it took about ten seconds for the postal worker to ask if we were sisters. This time, we didn't coo or play in response like we used to—though, I was ready and hoping we might. Instead, I could tell my friend was irked. She gave a polite smile, said no, and went on with her business.

My friend was on a special diet at the time of my visit, one she went off shortly after I left, so we ate breakfast at a vegan spot, and she pointed out ¿Por Qué No? where she said I could go for tacos alone. We went to Powell's on Hawthorne to browse and sip and sit, but instead of catching up, she got a diet book and told me about all the things we shouldn't be putting in our bodies—one of them, the coffee I was drinking as she sipped herbal tea. Next, she took me to another café where I was increasingly self-conscious about the coffee (my third of the day) and muffin I ordered. We sat outside in the sun together, eyes closed and heads tilted back. She started asking about my family and, eventually, my grandmother specifically.

"So, she didn't even speak Spanish?" she asked.

At that point, I didn't know my grandmother wasn't allowed to learn Spanish as a girl. I hadn't yet spit into a vial for AncestryDNA, a Christmas gift from my mother, and been shown Sonora as the region of our more recent generations. I didn't know how to explain the whitewashing effect of US military culture that went back generations on both sides of my family. I didn't know how to explain that my grandmother descended from addicts and abusers and didn't like to talk about her past or where she came from.

"I didn't realize your *grandmother* didn't even speak Spanish," she said, and I could see her wheels turning as others' and my own often do when considering my ethnicity, gauging proximity to determine how big a piece of me this facet represents and whether or not it's enough for me to claim.

"In that case," she started again, "I'd encourage you to tread *very* carefully." I could see her bricking up the space between us. "Don't go around calling yourself a Chicana and shit," and in that moment, I understood the trip we'd planned for what it was: a dream.

Our last stop was a resale shop where—surprisingly, after our talk at the café—things felt the most normal between us they had all day, at least for a while. We loaded our arms with clothes and hefted piles to the fitting rooms, picking things out for each other and swapping as we went. I got to the huipil in my stack and stepped out from behind the curtain to show her as I'd done with every outfit prior. The dress was thick and clearly handmade and stitched. I felt strong and beautiful in it, connected to the women who came before me. I bought the dress that day knowing I'd save it for something special and eventually wore it for the first time almost two years later on my wedding day with a grocery-store bouquet and a pair of earrings from my grandmother. When the curtain opened, my friend's face took on the same look it had at the post office when we'd been asked if we were sisters.

"Nice," was all she said.

About
the Author

Brenna Womer is a queer, childfree, Latine prose writer and poet. She is the author of *Honeypot* (Spuyten Duyvil, 2019) and two chapbooks. Her work has appeared in *North American Review*, *Redivider*, *Indiana Review*, *The Normal School*, and elsewhere. She is an Assistant Professor of Creative Writing and teaches in the MFA program at California State University in Fresno, where she lives with her two rescue pit bulls.

FLOWERSONG
PRESS

FlowerSong Press nurtures essential verse
from, about, and throughout the
borderlands. Literary. Lyrical. Boundless.

Sign up for announcements about
new and upcoming titles at:

www.flowersongpress.com

www.ingramcontent.com/pod-product-compliance
Lightning Source LLC
Chambersburg PA
CBHW031246120626
46545CB00007B/2675